MARINE AQUARIA

Clownfishes, or anemonefishes as they are sometimes called, get
along perfectly well with their anemones.

Live corals do well in the aquarium, but beginners are much better off with the dead, dried and bleached corals since they are not tank polluters.

rather small almost jelly-like ball. This is what you are bringing home with assurances that it will, with proper attention, blossom out into its beautiful shape again. As you put this blob (that's what it looks like) into the tank it will sink slowly to the bottom and lie there for a while, making you wonder what you did wrong. Eventually, however, it will start to relax and expand, moving along on its basal disc to a position on some coral, a rock, or even the glass side of the aquarium where it senses that the current, light, or whatever is just right. Soon it will have become its old self again, sitting there waving its tentacles in search of food. Most anemones are suitable for an invertebrate aquarium, although *Cerianthus* and some of its relatives are very toxic and can kill other anemones and coral by contact.

Corals have been kept alive in some aquaria, but in general they do not do well at all. More success has been achieved with the large-polyp species than with the small-polyp species and with the reef flat or tidal pool species than the stronger current reef corals. One of the commonest decorations for marine tanks is the cured white skeleton of the staghorn coral, *Acropora* species. Yet the living *Acropora* is one of the hardest to keep. It exudes a great deal of mucus when unhappy and can foul a tank very rapidly when it dies.

Few worms ever make it into the invertebrate aquarium. There are some brilliantly colored flatworms, but they seem to disintegrate just by looking at them. Featherduster worms are generally available (often as part of a "living rock") and are quite attractive. Since they are borers you have to take the coral rock along with them.

There are always new invertebrates that show up from time to time which nobody seems to know anything about. These are generally to be avoided unless you are absolutely sure they will not turn out to be terrors in the tank, destroying everything they can.

Invertebrates are treated in much the same way as the fishes, as far as bagging them and bringing them home. Many must be handled a little more carefully than the fishes or they might become damaged on the trip. Usually only one per plastic bag is the limit. Check the water chemistry as you do with the fishes and adjust it accordingly. Place the attached or semi-attached invertebrates in the aquarium first, allowing time for the anemones to crawl around until they find their spot. They will probably wander around a bit later but will stay put when placed in a tank in the initially selected spot. Then add the territorial species and finally the rovers or wanderers. After a while everybody gets settled down and your aquarium starts to look just the way you planned it—at least until all the animals decide they like one side of the tank instead of the other and you have one crowded end and one empty end. In such a case try to find out why they all want the one end of the aquarium. Perhaps the filter inlet or outlet is there or the airstone might provide better aeration at one end of the tank; the light may be too bright in one place or the tank may be too dark in another. Changing the tank situation will probably have an effect on the distribution of your animals. Once you have learned the cause and effect you can pretty well guide the invertebrates to where you want them.

An ideal, easy-to-maintain tank is one that is large (the larger, the better), preferably 135 gallons (about 400 liters) or more, with lots of open space in the center.

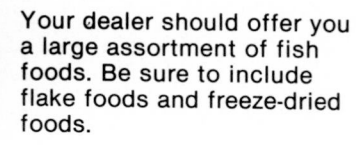
Your dealer should offer you a large assortment of fish foods. Be sure to include flake foods and freeze-dried foods.

Feeding

Feeding marine animals used to be a very difficult proposition. The available foods were few and far between and not of the greatest quality. You had to feed brine shrimp almost exclusively, adding whichever of the freshwater fish and invertebrate foods you could get your animals to eat. Now there are more and more foods specifically designed and packaged for marine fishes. There are frozen foods that include squid, shrimps, krill, etc., as well as marine plankton. Mixed with some of the packaged frozen foods are various types of vegetable matter like kelp or other algae for the herbivorous or omnivorous species. This does not mean that brine shrimp should be forgotten. Brine shrimp in almost any form is an excellent food for most marine animals.

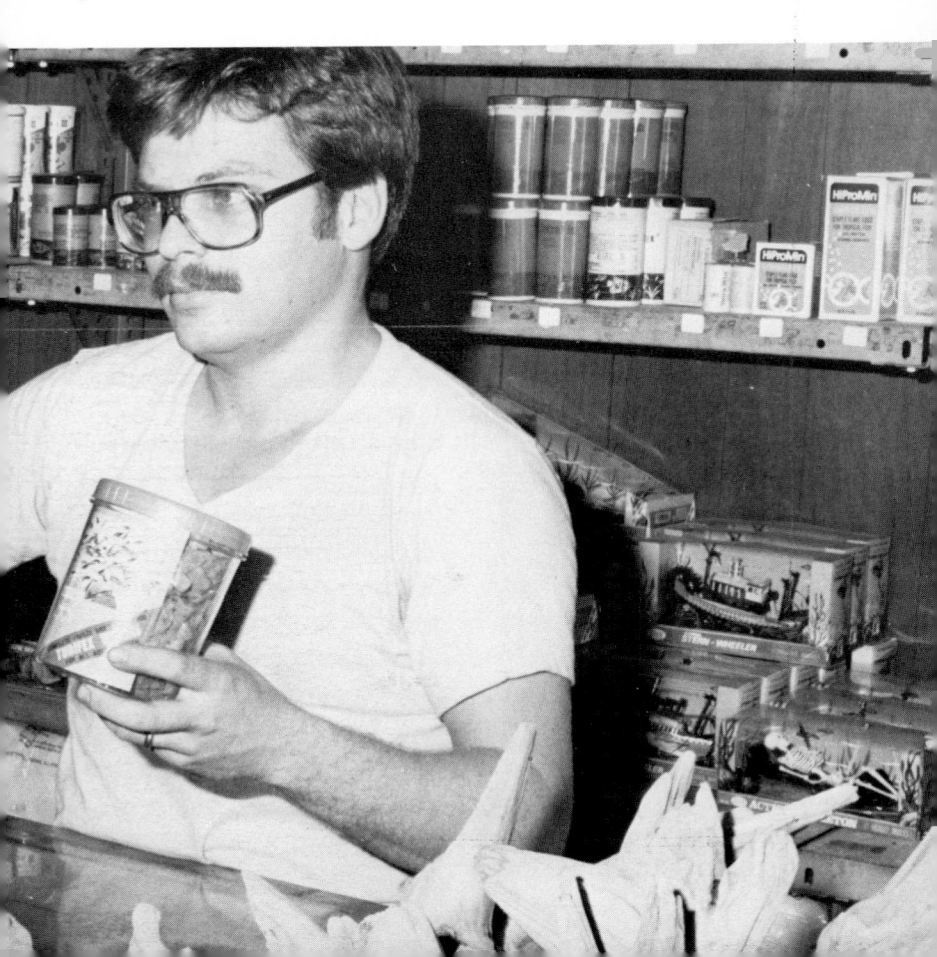

An aquarium can be built into an old television cabinet or even into a hand-made cabinet as this one is. But be sure there is suitable access to clean and service the tank.

The famous Belgian photographer Guy van den Bossche is both an aquarist and avid collector of shells. His tanks are always filled with interesting shells. Photo by Guy v.d. Bossche.

You must be aware of how and what your animals eat if you are to be successful in keeping them well fed and happy. For example, dropping in some frozen food that sinks to the bottom on the opposite end of the tank from an anemone does the anemone no good whatever. With its limited powers of locomotion it probably couldn't get to the food before it was eaten by one of the other inhabitants of the tank. Feeding fast-moving live food does not make sense when the animals you have in the tank are slow-moving types that can't catch it.

Active fishes are generally no problem as far as their being able to catch the food offered. Quite the opposite—you will have a problem keeping some of the food away from the faster fishes so that the slower ones get their share. Often you just have to wait until the fast fishes are full and ignore the food, although they may just play with it or chase it just because the other fishes show interest in it. The same with invertebrates. There are quick-moving ones that are able to get to the food first and hog it all to themselves. You just have to wait until they finish before giving food to the slower species. Certain animals must be fed individually or they might starve. Sea anemones, for example, must be fed with an eyedropper or similar device (basters have been used successfully) or there must be moving food (live brine shrimp for example) that comes within reach of their tentacles.

Filter-feeders (bivalves, featherduster worms, etc.) are a bit more difficult to feed. The best method is to have a current of water carry food items to them as happens in nature. This may not be very easy to do in the aquarium, but it can be managed with the use of airstones or outlets from power filters. If the current carries the food-laden water over the filter-feeders before the rest of the inhabitants are able to get to it, you will have the best of all situations. The filter-feeders get their food and you have a clean-up squad waiting to see that there are no leftovers to foul the tank. Some people advocate removing the filter-feeders from the tank and placing

Marine Aquaria

Dr. Warren E. Burgess

Fishes are fun . . . and funny. They are interesting and entertaining to watch and to care for.

Marine aquaria are expensive.
They are not recommended
for children as they are too
complicated to care for.

Introduction

To be able to maintain some of the exotic marine creatures that inhabit the world's oceans in home aquaria has been a dream of many individuals. This dream may have been initiated by seeing these animals on a vacation trip involving snorkeling on a reef, on a visit to one of the large commercial aquariums that have on exhibit tanks of marine fishes or invertebrates, or while viewing the marine tanks in a local pet shop. The feeling is generally enhanced by visits to friends or acquaintances who have already succeeded in setting up beautiful marine aquaria. When the urge to actually do

something about this dream finally becomes strong enough, there is the devouring of book after book on the subject along with visits to the local aquarium shops that sell marine fishes and invertebrates to check out some of the species that are available and to price some of the equipment needed to get started.

The person who gets involved with the marine hobby is not necessarily a "graduate" of freshwater fishkeeping, although this is often the case. As a matter of fact, some freshwater aquarists are primarily interested in breeding their fishes and could care less about the marine hobby, where there is little chance of spawning success. But with the increasing number of successful spawnings in the marine field, even these aquarists are being attracted to saltwater animals. The greatest attraction of the marine aquarium, however, does not seem to be the possibility of spawning the animals but is a combination of the beauty of the animals themselves and their interesting habits or behavior. There is still a challenge for those who wish to tackle the more difficult species, and for those who have little or no experience there are species that are relatively easy to keep. The array of animal life suitable for keeping in home aquaria is so vast there is undoubtedly something for everyone.

Are the time, effort, and expense worth it? Nobody but you can answer that question. Is it possible to put a value on the feeling of satisfaction and contentment you get while sitting in front of your own marine aquarium housing strange and beautiful fishes or invertebrates, watching their antics and proudly showing them off to your friends?

To get started with marine aquaria requires the locating of a specialist dealer. Don't buy marine aquaria, marine fishes or supplies from a five-and-dime operation as they do not have suitably trained personnel who can help you AFTER the sale.

Your dealer should special-
ize in marine aquaria. If he
does, he'll have all the
things you'll need to get
started properly.

Getting Started—
The Essentials

them in a smaller receptacle where there is food-laden water. When feeding is finished the filter-feeders are returned to their original tank. This is a difficult, often messy, project that takes a bit of time and may cause damage to the animals. It does accomplish the prime objective of feeding the animals, however.

The size of the food is important. Large crabs can eat adult brine shrimp but have a hard time with the baby brine. They do much better on a larger piece of shrimp or fish which they can manipulate with their claws. Groupers can swallow whole fishes, but damselfishes do better on smaller items like the brine shrimps. Butterflyfishes and angelfishes have small mouths that are used for eating tiny animals or for nibbling away at larger pieces of food, taking little bits at a time.

Basically you must choose the food sizes and types that suit your particular animals. For this you need to know a bit about their feeding habits. The information can usually be found in any of the books that treat the animals species by species, or it can be had from your dealer. Your dealer has been keeping the species in his tanks and undoubtedly has them on a diet that he has had success with.

You might keep the feeding types in mind when selecting the animals that will be housed in your tanks. It is easier to feed the same type of food to all your charges than to try and have a special diet for each and every species. You will be surprised how many different species will be able to thrive on a similar diet. Once you have your animals eating regularly and growing (or at least putting on weight) and you feel that they will do even better with a more varied and nutritious diet, you might then try some additional foods. If they are rejected you can always go back to the old diet.

The frequency of feeding depends upon the species of animals kept. Some small active fishes burn up a lot of energy and require several feedings each day. Other species may need only one large piece of food each week. Again, refer to the write-ups of individual species for specific information.

1

2

It just takes a little ingenuity! Your marine aquarium can be used as a table for your bar (1), as a room divider in the kitchen (2) or even as a living wall in a restaurant (3), or if you are really clever, perhaps built into your bathroom surrounding a bathtub (4).

Then have your dealer net them and hold them close to the glass for visual inspection. Check them in the bag before you leave the store.

Selecting marine invertebrates is not as simple as selecting marine fishes. You'll need help from the dealer.

ing and run it from the tank to the bucket. Place a clamp on the tubing. Start a siphoning action from the tank to the tray regulated by the clamp to a bit more than a trickle. As aquarium water slowly flows into the bucket the fish will have a chance to get acclimated to it. There will be no sudden shock. As the bucket starts to fill some water can be dipped out from time to time and returned to the aquarium. Many wholesalers use this method for newly arrived fishes that they wish to acclimate to their own water conditions after their long journey. Remember to keep an eye on your filters to see that the aquarium water level does not go down so far as to cause them to run dry. There is no set time for this water exchange. The time depends on the rate of flow through the tubing, the differences in pH and other factors between the two waters, and the tolerances of the fishes themselves. Tolerances range from species that might go into shock at the slightest difference between the two types of water to those that could adapt immediately if just dumped into the aquarium without any adjustment whatever. If you have a mixture of hardy and delicate fishes be sure to accom-

modate the more delicate ones. The best way to determine when to place the fishes in the tank is to keep checking the water with the fishes to see when the chemistry is equivalent to the tank water. When you are satisfied that they are sufficiently equal, the fishes can be placed in the tank. The water can be returned to its proper level in the main tank and any adjustments made in the chemistry in case the water that the fishes were carried home in caused a change.

Now is the first time that you can really relax and enjoy your aquarium. The fishes might take a little time to adjust to their new surroundings, but pretty soon they will not hide among the coral as much or dash wildly around the tank when anybody approaches. Eventually you will be allowed to approach and view your tank without having to sneak up on it to see all the inhabitants. Your fishes might even get to recognize you (especially if you are the one to feed them) and come to the front of the tank at your approach. This is one point where you really get a lot of satisfaction from your aquarium.

SELECTING INVERTEBRATES

Selecting invertebrates for a marine aquarium is not as simple as selecting fishes. There are so many different types it is hard to describe all the combinations of animals that are possible. You have to be careful about which animals will live with which. Placing an octopus in an aquarium with a crab means death to the crab, as it is one of the natural food items of the octopus. Similarly, some starfishes feed on bivalves (scallops and clams); there are carnivorous gastropods (snails) that hunt other animals (including other gastropods and even fishes); the shrimp *Hymenocera* will dine on starfishes; and most of the swimming crabs will attack anything in sight. I have seen one of the swimming crabs *(Callinectes)* in a tank with some fish try desperately to grab the fish as they swam past. In this case the situation was almost comical, for the fish looked almost big enough to eat the crab and

(1) Inspect your purchase (fish or invertebrate) carefully when it is confined in the net to see if it is healthy. (2) Try to buy fishes that can live in peace with your invertebrates if you wish to keep both in the same tank. (3) It is possible to have both fishes and invertebrates together ... crustaceans, starfishes, anemones, and molluscs are the most commonly kept invertebrates.

if the crab ever got hold of the fish I am sure it would have been given a rather rough ride about the tank until it let go.

One of the most common invertebrates kept in home marine aquaria is the banded coral shrimp or cleaning shrimp, *Stenopus hispidus.* On the reef it will hide under a ledge or in a cave with only its four brilliant white antennae sticking out. This is a signal to passing fish that if they stop and pose it will come out and deftly remove parasites, dead tissue, or other unwanted material from them. They will do this in an aquarium, and some experienced aquarists keep them in their fish tanks so that any fishes needing cleaning can get it done. For this service the fishes do not eat the little shrimp—at least not very often. Actually the *Stenopus* may get along better with the fish than they would with another of their own kind. It has often occurred that a novice aquarist who has succeeded in keeping one of these shrimps picks up another to "pair them up." Unfortunately when the two meet they will generally attempt to tear each other apart. Only one to a tank please, unless you get a true mated pair already living together in your dealer's tank.

Besides *Stenopus* there are many other shrimps available for your invertebrate aquarium. They come in all shapes and colors and are usually quite hardy. In fact, as they grow you might get a surprise one morning in the aquarium by seeing two identical shrimps when there was only one before. If you look closely, however, you will see that one of the shrimps is completely hollow. This is a molted skin that is shed by a shrimp at intervals to allow it to grow. The shrimp's covering is rigid and restricts the shrimp (and other crustaceans as well) from growing larger. It is therefore molted from time to time, and each time the shrimp increases its size before its new covering hardens like the old one. This "soft-shelled" stage is a very vulnerable one for a crustacean, and you might keep a wary eye on the tank when you know the molting stage is near.

Nudibranches (sea-slugs) are very beautiful shell-less snails

If the anemones are too large they might kill the fishes in the tank by stinging them with their poisonous tentacles.

that are ever-present in dealers' tanks. They are so beautiful that it is very hard not to bring one back now and then. But they are very difficult to keep for a long time since it is almost impossible to find the right food for them. Although a few might survive by scraping algae from the decorations, most are predators on such things as bryozoans, corals, or other nudibranchs, foods very hard to maintain in aquaria. A tank with a good growth of sessile invertebrates might keep them going for a while, but they eventually lack something vital and die.

Anemones are favorites and make interesting additions to an invertebrate aquarium (as well as the aforementioned clownfish-anemone combination). There are problems, but with care you can usually set up one or more in your tank without too much trouble. When you purchase an anemone, watch the dealer get it out of his tank. He will tickle or worry the base of the anemone until it peels off the glass or rock to which it is attached. By this time it has contracted into a

Corals kept in a tank eventually turn brownish (above) and must be cleaned to return them to their original color (below).

If your fish become ill, contact your dealer immediately. If possible bring in the fish, or invite him to see the sick fish in your home.

Diseases and Ailments

It is not the objective of this book to discuss the various diseases or other problems that may affect the health and well-being of your animals. There are a number of good books available devoted to diagnosing troubles and treating injuries and ailments. I will just give you a few hints on what to do when something goes wrong.

If you have followed all the procedures correctly and carefully and have set up the tanks properly, your animals should be doing just fine. You should be able to sit in front of your aquaria and watch your "pets" go through their normal daily routines. It is when one or more of them break the usual routine and start to act in an unusual manner that you

The *Pomacanthus semicirculatus* shown above is suffering from an attack of *Cryptocaryon* infection as evidenced by the white blotches. On the facing page is a *Monodactylus sebae* with a similar infection, but this one was caused by *Henneguya*. There are books on marine aquarium fish diseases and their cures, but ask your dealer for first aid help as soon as possible.

If diseases plague your aquarium, start all over. New gravel, new fishes, new water and a completely sterilized tank.

have to start checking to see exactly what is happening. This unusual behavior may be a normal phase in that particular species' life or some behavior related to spawning, aggression, or other temporary phenomena. But all too often it means something is wrong and if not corrected will eventually lead to the death of that individual or everything in the entire tank.

Look for erratic behavior such as sudden starts or jumps or scratching on the coral decorations or sand. Look for clamped fins or hiding in a corner or under one of the decorations. Watch to see if the individual eats properly, has gone on a hunger strike, or is getting too thin in spite of eating. Check to see if there are obvious manifestations of some injury or disease such as ragged fins, white spots on the body or fins, lesions or other sores, pop-eyes, unusual growths on some part of the body or redness at the fin bases or other parts of the body where it shouldn't be. If any of these symptoms occur in your animals, check it out in one of the disease books or ask your dealer.

Check your water chemistry, temperature, etc., to see if everything is as it should be. Make sure no metals have come in contact with your aquarium water and check to see that no toxic fumes (from painting, spraying for insects, cigarette smoking, etc.) have been pumped into the tank by your pump. Change some of the water to see if that helps (perhaps the trace elements have become depleted).

Look for as many clues as you can to try and reason out what is wrong. For example, a parasite might affect only one animal, or a disease may start with one animal and spread rapidly to the others; poison in the tank usually affects all the inhabitants at the same time (although often to different degrees depending upon their individual tolerance levels). Maybe one animal's erratic behavior might be due to aggressiveness on the part of one of its tankmates. Even when the animals are carefully chosen there might be an aggressive individual that keeps one or more of the others in constant fear for their lives.

A word to the wise. When you want to add new fishes or invertebrates to your tank, quarantine them for a couple of weeks. You can watch them to see that they are behaving normally, eating well, and showing no signs of parasites or diseases. There are many tales of woe in which a particular animal couldn't be resisted and when brought home was dumped into the community tank. In a short while the new arrival was showing signs of some disease that immediately spread through the tank, causing grief to the owner as he fought to save as many lives as possible. The stress of shipping or moving will generally weaken an animal, and if there are disease organisms present they may get a head start in attacking that animal. A period of quarantine will not only give you time to see if it has contracted any disease but will also give you time to acclimate it to your conditions so it becomes strong enough to take its place in the community tank without any trouble.

CONTENTS

All photographs by Dr. Herbert R. Axelrod unless otherwise credited. The models are Mike Fishman and Karen Farrell.

ISBN 0-87666-533-4

© 1980 by T.F.H. Publications, Inc. Ltd.

Distributed in the UNITED STATES by T.F.H. Publications, Inc., 211 West Sylvania Avenue, Neptune City, NJ 07753; in CANADA by H & L Pet Supplies Inc., 27 Kingston Crescent, Kitchener, Ontario N2B 2T6; Rolf C. Hagen Ltd., 3225 Sartelon Street, Montreal 382 Quebec; in ENGLAND by T.F.H. (Great Britain) Ltd., 11 Ormside Way, Holmethorpe Industrial Estate, Redhill, Surrey RH1 2PX; in AUSTRALIA AND THE SOUTH PACIFIC by T.F.H. (Australia) Pty. Ltd., Box 149, Brookvale 2100 N.S.W., Australia; in NEW ZEALAND by Ross Haines & Son, Ltd., 18 Monmouth Street, Grey Lynn, Auckland 2 New Zealand; in SINGAPORE AND MALAYSIA by MPH Distributors Pte., 71-77 Stamford Road, Singapore 0617; in the PHILIPPINES by Bio-Research, 5 Lippay Street, San Lorenzo Village, Makati, Rizal; in SOUTH AFRICA by Multipet Pty. Ltd., 30 Turners Avenue, Durban 4001. Published by T.F.H. Publications Inc., Ltd., the British Crown Colony of Hong Kong. THIS IS THE 1983 EDITION.

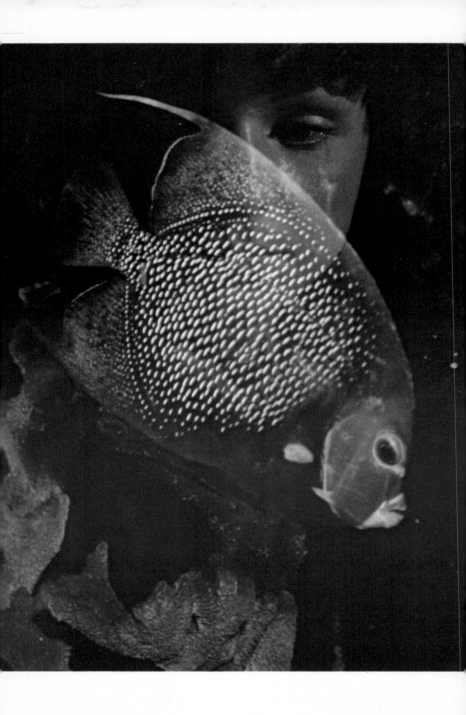

Index

Transposing an idea or dream into reality often takes a lot of planning and organization. You may regret it if you blindly run out to the store and buy a lot of equipment, set it up, and then wonder what animals to buy. That is putting the proverbial cart before the horse. It is best to first have a good idea of what you want in a marine aquarium, then you can go out and look for the proper equipment to handle it. Your decisions may have to be modified by information supplied by your pet shop owner or manager, but at least you will be able to make the alterations to your ideas intelligently.

THE AQUARIUM

Once you have decided on the animals you want to keep (and can keep), the next major decisions are the type of tank to buy, its size, its support, and its location.

The type of tank recommended is the all-glass aquarium. In recent years this type of aquarium has come into its own. Of new tanks purchased for either freshwater or marine animals, almost all of them are of the all-glass type. These consist of four glass sides and a glass bottom cemented together with a silicone sealant. At first many aquarists built their own all-glass tanks since the prices for ready-made tanks were often exceedingly high and it was a relatively simple matter to put one together. But the prices on manufactured tanks have dropped so drastically since they first appeared on the market that it no longer pays to take the time or trouble to build your own unless you need a special size or shape.

It is not recommended that you try to modify an old metal-framed tank for marine use. Although it can be done, it is a risky proposition at best, and the possible loss of fish from metal or other poisoning would be greater than the cost of a new all-glass aquarium.

The size of the tank depends primarily upon what animals are to be kept. For some fishes and invertebrates a small tank will be sufficient, but for general fishkeeping (or invertebrate keeping) nothing smaller than 25 gallons should be considered. Fifty- to 125-gallon aquaria are more likely to be selected by the knowledgeable aquarist. He knows this larger capacity gives him more freedom in selecting the animals he would like to keep and more time to correct the situation if something goes awry. Once you have mastered the marine techniques with a 50-gallon aquarium, you can try the smaller ones for specialty fishes or invertebrates.

SUPPORT FOR YOUR TANK

There are many different kinds of aquarium stands, varying from simple black metal rod constructions to quite fancy

wood-grain or simulated wood-grain foundations with matching hoods. These latter stands usually have a cabinet below for storage of accessories such as nets, siphon tubes, food, spare parts, or whatever. There are usually no initial problems with good quality commercially built stands, and they are constructed to fit exactly the commercially built aquaria. Stands supporting marine tanks must be checked frequently for rust as the corrosive action of salt water is many times worse than that of fresh water. And no matter how careful you are, there are always some times when water is spilled or a few drops run down the sides of the tank and reach the stand. Even the air in the immediate vicinity of the tank is more saturated with salt and can have an effect on the metal stands.

Strength is also very important in stands. The commercial stands are built to take the stresses of the normal tanks and will support the weight of the water, coral, etc., with no trouble. For those who want to build their own supports for their tanks, remember that salt water is heavy (about 8½ pounds per gallon) and a 50-gallon tank thus contains water weighing about 425 pounds. Add to this the weight of the gravel, coral decorations, and tank itself and you have an idea of what weight the stand must support. When considering the larger tanks of 125 gallons or so you are talking about over 1,000 pounds of water alone. That's more than half a ton! Start adding the weight of the gravel, decorations, etc., and you not only have to consider the strength of the stand but also of the floor the tank will be standing on. For these larger tanks you might be wise to consult someone knowledgeable in construction, or better yet structural engineering, for advice on whether your floor can support the weight.

Materials for stands vary depending upon the size of the tank and the esthetic demands of the aquarist. Some aquarists are satisfied with a commercial black metal stand, others the fancier wood-grained models, and still others use cement blocks in combination with heavy wooden boards. The ce-

The size and kind of aquarium you purchase will be limited only by the amount of space you have available—and the money you want to invest. The least expensive tank is a rectangular wood-grained aquarium. The tank on the facing page is much more expensive.

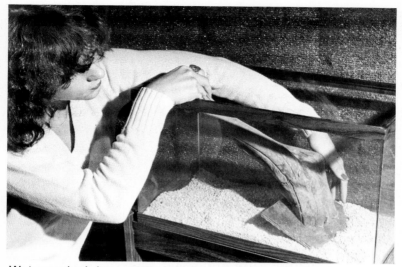
Water-soaked logs make good, inexpensive decorations. They should be added to the tank as soon as the sand is put in.

ment block stands can be left as is or covered on the front and sides by a cloth or even wood paneling. For those on an unlimited budget specially constructed bases such as those used for room dividers or integrated into part of the wall can be considered. The important factor is strength, beauty having to be relegated to a secondary consideration.

LOCATION OF THE TANK

Aside from the necessity to locate your tank on a suitably sturdy floor, other considerations must be taken into account. First of all is the light. Placing your tank where it receives direct sunlight for several hours a day will cause the water to turn green rather quickly. The heat from the sun in the summertime may also cause problems by pushing the temperature in the tank up beyond the comfort zone for the animals—perhaps even to a lethal level. This same problem may be encountered if the tank is placed near a heater such as a radiator. A cold draft from a window, door, or air conditioner will not be as troublesome if the tank is supplied with

its own heater(s), but it is best to avoid such placement of the tank in case the chill from the cold air is too much for the heaters to handle. Even if the heater(s) can keep the water at the proper temperature level, the cool air will cause them to run almost continuously, leading to an early breakdown of the heater and higher electric bills.

It is best to place a tank in a spot where there is a moderate amount of light, an even temperature, and where there are bound to be people around some of the time. This last suggestion is to help the animals to become conditioned to the presence of people so that they do not run and hide every time you enter the room. Don't forget to place the tank within a reasonable distance of an electrical outlet (to run the pumps, lights, etc.) unless the locality is so good you would rather run an extension cord to the tank rather than select a less suitable place.

With the aquarium in place actual setting up can proceed. The first operations include adding the water, bottom gravel, and any bottom type filters.

Study tank setups at your aquarium store and get some ideas as to how you'd like your own tank to look.

A reliable dealer will have a wide variety of fishes to choose from and be able to bag them properly for your trip home (facing page). He will have a range of equipment from different manufacturers to be sure to suit your needs and a wealth of literature which will help you learn about the animals you expect to keep.

THE WATER

There are two basic ways of providing your aquarium with water in which the fishes and invertebrates can live. The first way is to use natural sea water which you can collect yourself; the second is to use one of the prepackaged marine water mixes currently on the market. If you collect your own water there are certain things to keep in mind. You must get the cleanest water possible, which normally entails traveling by boat out into the ocean and loading up your containers there. The containers should be of such material so as not to contaminate the water. Metal buckets, for example, should be avoided. There are several types of 5-gallon plastic or glass containers that are excellent for this purpose. Glass is safer chemically than plastic, but there is the disadvantage of its fragility; additionally, glass carboys commonly have metal caps. New plastic containers should be cured by filling them with sea water, letting them stand for a couple of weeks, and then dumping out the water. This removes the "newness." Many containers do not need this curing, but if you are not sure it is better to be safe and do it this way. You can also check your water source in this way. After several weeks of storage you can test the water to see what changes have occurred. If you end up with a smelly batch of water you had better locate a different source. Once your containers are safe for use and the water source is okay, you can begin collecting for your aquaria. Collect more water than you need for your present set-up of tanks. It is always good to have enough water for a complete change in all your tanks. If this is not practical, enough extra water for a complete change in at least one or two of the tanks is recommended. If anything goes wrong you can switch the fishes and invertebrates from the foul water into clean water immediately. Use common sense in collecting the water. For instance, do not draw the water from right next to the motor, exhaust outlets, or other areas where oil or grease could contaminate it.

Since natural sea water contains living organisms, it is best

to filter it before storage. This can be done simply by pouring it through a clean handkerchief. You will be amazed by the material, living or otherwise, that remains behind in the handkerchief. The living material is mostly plankton, which is present in almost all sea water in greater or lesser quantities. A bit of the handkerchief residue placed in a small watchglass and viewed under a low power microscope is a sight to behold. There may be larval forms of many animals including fishes, crustaceans, echinoderms, worms, as well as eggs of various species or fully grown animals such as copepods. Each sample may contain something new and excitingly different. Much of the plankton will die in the water and pollute it if not removed. If the plankton is plentiful the water will eventually become too foul for the fishes or invertebrates to ever live in it and will have to be discarded. It is best then to filter out as much organic material as possible before storage. Storage is generally accomplished by placing the containers in a darkened area. This prevents the plants from reproducing. It is very discouraging to find that your supply of clean water has turned green from an algal bloom caused by a high nutrient level (the dead plankton supplying the nutrients) and plenty of light for photosynthesis.

"Natural" sea water has been offered to marine aquarists in the past, but more recently the cost of shipping the filtered water has become prohibitive when compared to the relatively safe and easy method of mixing prepackaged salts. The idea of setting up a tank of Red Sea fishes, for example, with water collected from the Red Sea itself sounds great but is impractical and not even necessary.

Synthetic sea water, prepared by using one of the commercial packages of "sea salts," has become the accepted medium in which to keep marine fishes. The earlier synthetic salts were not very good, and an aquarist had almost a better chance to keep his fishes alive by carting home ocean water than to trust them to the concoctions that were available. Much of the problem was due to the lack of what are called

Your fish must be carefully tended when they are first brought
home. Allow the bag to float in your home aquarium for 15 minutes
or so (1) to bring the temperature to the proper level. By closing the
hood cover on the edge of the bag you can position it so you don't
have to hold it (2). After 15 minutes, pour the contents (3) into the
aquarium.

trace elements. The first marine salts formulas were based on the major constituents of sea water with little regard for the trace elements. The idea was that these trace elements were in such infinitesimally small amounts that leaving them out wouldn't matter. In some cases this was true, but there are trace elements that are apparently essential to the well-being of both invertebrates and fishes, and various invertebrates may need different trace elements than the fishes. Through the years, partly by trial and error and partly by analysis, the formulas for marine salts have been improved so that several of those on the market are considered safe to use. They are not as good as good clean ocean water, as some experiments have indicated, but are suitable enough for properly kept aquaria. It is only when pollution levels are high that the synthetic salts fall short of the capabilities of natural sea water. Fishes in properly kept aquaria with synthetic sea water have been known to live for many years, with their ultimate demise not attributable to the water.

Synthetic sea water has certain advantages. The salts are easily packaged and shipped so that hobbyists in inland areas, as well as those along the coasts who cannot (or do not wish to) collect their own sea water, can make use of them. The resulting water is free from plankton and other undesirable matter and is quite consistent in composition. Water changes are thus made relatively simply with water that is almost identical to the original (some changes will occur in the water chemistry with animals living in it). And, if there is a catastrophe in one of your tanks, a complete change of water is possible with synthetic salts without too much delay or trauma to the animals. It is best then to keep a supply of marine mix handy for emergencies.

When mixing the synthetic salts be sure to follow the instructions carefully. Several of the major synthetic salts are mixed differently; for example, one might be a straight one-step affair while another might entail mixing the solution in stages. Whatever the case, do not mix the salts directly in

your aquarium. Use a separate container of glass or non-toxic plastic for mixing (plastic garbage pails have been used successfully). If it can be marked off according to number of gallons at certain levels so much the better.

Although most of the synthetic salts are usable almost immediately after they are mixed (as soon as the water turns clear), some require a little ageing. This could mean an hour or two of standing to up to 24 hours ageing combined with mild aeration. It might be a good practice to age all newly mixed water just to be safe.

Can one mix different types of synthetic salts? Although some manufacturers claim this is not possible, the formulas are so close there should be no problem. No experimental evidence is available that would prove or disprove the different claims.

The synthetic salts are buffered so that a pH reading of about 8.3 is obtained with proper mixing. If your pH values are quite different from those expected, check the directions to be sure that you have the proper proportions of mix and water. Also check your tap water to see if it would be of such a different pH that the solution would be affected. When all such avenues are exhausted, go back to the store where you purchased the salts and inquire as to what might have gone wrong.

The salinity should also come out to a value near that of normal sea water (usually considered as 34 o/oo [=parts per thousand]). The salinity can be determined through use of a standard hydrometer. The hydrometer measures the specific gravity of the water, which may be defined as the ratio of the weight of a given volume of sea water to the weight of an equal volume of distilled water. The weight of sea water is dependent upon the amount of salts it contains; therefore the hydrometer reading can be used to determine the salinity. Hydrometers are normally calibrated to read correctly at 15° C. Water warmer than 15° C. will be less dense than that at 15° C. and water cooler than 15° C. will be more dense.

Rely upon your aquarium shop specialist to guide you when purchasing corals. Keep in mind the size of your aquarium (facing page) when purchasing corals.

Tables are available for the adjustment of the hydrometer readings and eventual conversion to the salinity. Actually, marine aquarium literature almost always refers to the specific gravity so that only the initial correction due to temperature need be made.

THE SUBSTRATE

The substrate is very important in a marine aquarium. It affects the chemical composition of the water in many instances, determines the flow of water through an undergravel filter (when one is used), provides a medium for burrowing animals, and often is decorative in nature. The major chemical effect caused by the type of gravel selected is a change in the pH, or perhaps more properly stated a resistance to an acidification of the water. When a marine aquarium is first set up the pH is adjusted to a value of about 8.3. When the animals are added, the uneaten food that is not removed, the excreta, etc., tend to drive the pH of the water toward the acid end of the spectrum. Gravel of a calcareous nature (dolomite, crushed coral rock or oyster shells, limestones chips, etc.) counteracts this acidifying trend to some extent, helping to keep the pH at the proper level. One or more of these substances should be available at your local aquarium store (especially if they also deal in African Rift Lake cichlids which also require pH levels of 8.0 or above).

The size of the gravel is important as well. If you are setting up your tank with an undergravel filter you must have the proper size grains. If they are too small they will go through the slots of the filter and wind up at the bottom of the tank or get stuck in the slots themselves, thereby clogging up the filter. If they are too big they provide little or no filtering action. When you buy your undergravel filter you can also select the bottom material (with the help of the store owner or manager) that will best suit your purpose. Grains a few millimeters long work best in most set-ups. Purchase enough gravel to enable you to cover the filter to a depth of

about two to three inches. Too much or too little will cut down the filtering ability of your filter.

In addition to the mechanical considerations of gravel type and size, the type of animals kept must be taken into account when selecting gravel. If you will have burrowers in the tank make sure that the gravel is of a size that will let them burrow without endangering themselves because of sharp edges or too fine grains that might get into the gills. Generally burrowing animals and undergravel filters are not compatible.

The substrate or gravel is extremely important. The sand must be selected according to its use. Read this section of the book carefully.

The small filter shown to the left is useful when several are used in various corners of the tank. A suitable background (below) enhances the beauty of your aquarium.

Other Basic Equipment

FILTERS

Filtration is an important aspect of marine aquarium keeping. Regardless of how carefully you feed your animals, there will always be some leftovers or particles that remain in the tank due to sloppy eaters, etc., and there are the inevitable biological processes resulting in excreted material (feces, etc.). If these are left in the tank, decay results with the accompaniment of a buildup of bacteria. The decomposition materials are in some cases toxic, and they tend to cause the water to become acidic. Mechanical filtration will remove much of the material and help keep the bacterial

count down, but without further measures such filtration is not enough. Nevertheless, filtration is necessary and several types of filters or filter systems will be discussed below. The additional measures needed to supplement the filter systems will be treated later in this book.

Undergravel filters have already been mentioned briefly above. These are flat plates that fit over the entire bottom of the tank a short distance above it. The plates are perforated with slits or holes of a relatively small size but spaced out over the entire plate. The corners of the plate(s) are provided with air lifts. As the air lift operates, the water is drawn up the tube and returned to the tank at the surface. Since the water being pulled up the tubes comes from below the plates, replacement water is drawn through the plates from the "living quarters" of the tank. This means that with two to three inches of gravel covering the plates the water passing through the slits of the filter plates has in effect been filtered, the filtered material remaining behind in the sand or gravel. Although the most commonly seen undergravel filter has been described here, there are several variations on this basic design available including some using tubes instead of plates.

Power filters are filters that have the water pumped through the filtering medium by a motor that is a part of the filter itself rather than a separate unit involved in running other filters, airstones, etc. The power filter is usually either a normal filter box that is hung on the side of the tank with a motor attached or a cylindrical unit that contains the filtering medium but again provided with a motor. The effectiveness of the power filter depends on its size, the quantity and quality of the filter material, and the power of the motor running it.

Marine aquaria may be provided with an undergravel filter, a power filter, or both. The size and combination of filters needed to properly keep your tank in good condition is dependent upon the size of your tank and the animals you

keep in it. Some animals are much cleaner than others and need less filtration; some are rather messy and would keep the tank in a constantly dirty condition without adequate filtration. Again the advice received from a competent store manager or owner will go a long way in helping you get the proper equipment for your tank. If you read the labels on the box that the power filter comes in you will probably find much of the information you need. After all, the filter was designed for a certain purpose and it works best when used for that purpose.

HEATERS

Most of the animals that will be housed in your aquaria come from the tropical oceans of the world. They suffer when the temperature drops too far, falling prey to many of the diseases prevalent in marine aquaria. To avoid this problem, heaters should be installed. There are a variety of heaters available including those that are submergible, others that clip onto the side of the tank, some with thermostats, and others without. It is usually best to get one that clips onto the side of the tank and has an integral thermostat with a warning light. The size (wattage) will again depend upon the size of your tank and may be determined by reading the labels on the packaging or asking advice from your dealer.

The heater is easily installed. Place it in a position where there is some circulation of the water (to carry the heated water throughout the tank) but no spray from airstones, filters, etc. Do not plug the heater in if it is not in the water.

The temperature that should be maintained is about 25° C., although anywhere from 21-30° C. is usually adequate. If enough tanks are maintained, heating the aquarium room to the proper temperature will keep them all at the proper temperature together—providing adequate energy is available for this purpose. Here again the larger tanks are safer, for they will take a long time to cool down if some malfunction in the heating system occurs. This time gained may be enough to save your fishes or invertebrates.

Make sure that the heater clip and other metalic parts of the heater do not come in contact with the water. If possible coat metal parts with a non-toxic plastic spray to prevent them from being affected by the water.

AERATION AND PUMPS

In general, marine aquaria need aeration in the form of airstones. Aeration can be provided with a system similar to that used by freshwater aquarists—a small pump with plastic tubing leading to the airstone or to a valve which divides the pressure to run more than one airstone and filter. In a large tank an airstone at either end of the tank helps keep the water thoroughly mixed, preventing buildup of carbon dioxide or hot and cold areas due to water immediately around the heater not being circulated fast enough through the tank. Many power filters are provided with a return flow system that will aerate the water as it is being returned to the tank after being filtered. In such cases only one airstone (or none) would be necessary. The pumps needed to run the airstone(s) and filter(s) can be ordinary pumps just as long as they have the power to push enough air through the number of airstones you have decided upon and work the filters as well. Remember that in the larger, deeper tanks the water pressure at the bottom is considerable, so a fairly powerful pump is needed. You can see the effect if you have a small pump with an airstone attached and slowly drop the airstone into a deep tank. Near the surface the airstone has plenty of pressure to create a good bubble stream, but as it descends in the tank the bubbles will decrease. In some instances the pressure is so great the bubbles actually stop. On the other hand, a pump that is too powerful would have to have a bleeder valve where extra air pressure can be released harmlessly. Otherwise either the bubbles will be too violent (disrupting the tank and splattering salt water around) or the back pressure will cause problems with the operation of the pump. These things should be considered when selecting the type and size pump for your tank.

A suitable, reliable heater is essential. Don't save money on a heater! Get the best, and be sure it's guaranteed by the DEALER as well as the manufacturer. The same is true of all the mechanical apparatus you buy.

The pump for running your airstones and filters (other than the power filter which comes complete with a pump) is an important piece of equipment. After all, where would your tank be if you suddenly lost all your aeration and filtration? You must therefore look for a dependable, well-built pump that you can rely on to keep going (with proper maintenance) for many years. A spare pump is not a bad idea, although if you have properly maintained your tank you will have time to try to fix a broken pump or run out and buy a new one (providing stores are open when your pump decides to quit). If the pump stops because of an electrical failure it might be wise to have a spare battery-operated pump to hold you over until the electricity is restored.

Pumps generally come in two types, vibrator and piston pumps. Piston pumps are the more powerful of the two, but

the vibrator pumps are quieter. For marine aquaria a good piston pump would probably be your best bet. When purchasing the pump it will be to your benefit to pick up some spare parts such as a diaphragm or belt and some oil. These will come in handy if there is a breakdown of the pump at an inopportune time.

REFLECTOR AND COVER

In a heated tank evaporation is relatively high. This causes the salinity to rise and, if left unchecked, could cause problems for your more delicate animals. The salinity can be brought back to normal by adding tap water since it is mostly fresh water that evaporates, the salts being left behind. To keep the evaporation to a minimum a cover is commonly used on marine tanks and may even be considered a "must" item. The cover should be constructed of glass or a non-toxic plastic and should extend over the entire top of the tank but still allow space for heaters, filter tubes, etc. Commercial glass covers are available that fit perfectly and have the proper openings for your equipment. Some even have a hinged section to allow easy access to the tank for feeding and cleaning. A full cover has the added advantage of preventing your animals from escaping from the tank and dying somewhere in a dark corner. Moray eels and octopuses are masters at escape, and even a full cover may not prevent them from getting out. I have seen an octopus lift a cover that had a heavy weight on top (which was supposed to prevent it from doing just that) and slither out of the tank with ease.

A reflector is commonly used in conjunction with a full cover. These can house either incandescent or fluorescent lights, the choice being up to the aquarist. The incandescent bulb has the advantage of being initially less expensive but has the disadvantages of producing a great deal of heat and being more costly to operate. Fluorescent lights are cooler and less expensive to operate but cost more to buy. Incandescent light is a bit more pleasing to the eye, but fluorescent

lights come in a variety of colors which can show off your animals to great advantage. For example, the special light commonly used for the freshwater neon tetras or cardinal tetras can be used to illuminate similarly adorned marine animals such as the neon goby. Another type of fluorescent bulb is used for promoting the growth of algae since it gives off light rays at the proper point in the spectrum for plant growth.

The position of the reflector is also important. If situated at the back of the tank, it will promote algal growth along the back where it is mostly out of the way, but it will not show your animals off to best advantage. The light placed at the front of the tank shows the fish off better but promotes algal growth on the front glass of the tank where you least want it. A compromise of placing it in the center of the tank may work if you have a reflector that is not designed for hooking over the edge of your tank or otherwise unsuitable for such a position. Again the decision is up to you.

The reflector may be a combination reflector-cover, in which case the position of the light is predetermined. If you have a separate light and cover you will want to place the light on top of the glass cover. This will help prevent salt water from splashing up into the fixture and causing corrosion, a possible short circuit, or electric shock. Be careful with incandescent lights since the heat they produce can crack the glass cover. Keep them far enough away from the glass so that air can circulate between.

The length of time the lights should remain on depends upon the wattage used, the size of the aquarium, and what you wish to accomplish with the light. For simple viewing, the light may be left on for a long period of time only if the wattage is low. This prevents algal growth from running rampant. For promotion of algal growth you need more wattage and a longer period of time when the lights are on. This strong light also inhibits the growth of unwanted brown algae, a result of insufficient light. If you have placed your

motor driven pump/filter ONE

for fresh or salt water
pumps up to
120 gallons per hour
extra quiet

AQUOLOGY
POWER 1

motor driven pump/filter

A reliable dealer will set up your marine aquarium for you. Of course it will be without water, but you'll be able to visualize it much better. The power filter you purchase (facing page) must be powerful enough to produce a current in your aquarium, as well as to filter the water.

tank where it receives direct sunlight during the day you must compensate for this illumination by cutting back on the artificial light. The amount depends upon the size of the tank, the type of artificial light you have, and where you are situated geographically (you would get more light in a tropical area than in a northern area in the winter, for example).

DECORATIONS

The only other items you will need before setting up your aquarium are the decorations. Although these can be added later, it is much simpler and safer to place them in position as you set everything else up. If you add the water before the decorations you will have to calculate the volume of water that will be displaced by these decorations. It is much easier to place the decorations in first and then add the water. Also, the decorations might have some effect on the chemistry of the water and it would be better to have all these reactions happen at the same time rather than setting up the tank without the decorations, having it become balanced, and then adding the decorations and upsetting the balance again.

The appearance of your tank will be dependent upon how well it is decorated. This of course is left to your own personal abilities to work with the material available. You may want to set up a tank that is as much like the reef that the animals come from as possible, but there are restrictions. For example, you will have a great deal of difficulty trying to grow plants in the aquariums, and things like sea fans just cannot be added as they will foul the tank. This limits your selection of items considerably, but with what is available you can do a darn good job. I am not including such things as plastic divers or sea chests or sunken ships, which are so artificial and out of proportion to the size of the animals that they never seem to add anything to the tank. You might be able to do something with them—if so, good luck.

Then what is left? Your basic decoration will be the skeletons of the animals that built the reef in the first place, the

corals themselves. In almost every good marine aquarium store there will be a selection of corals. You can choose from delicate branching forms to heavy solid coral heads. A mixture of the various types of corals can make a very pleasing interior without need for additional decorations.

With the growth of the marine hobby manufacturers have come up with a variety of plastic items that can be used to help decorate marine tanks. There are various types of plastic marine seaweeds (algae) now available, copied from species from various parts of the world. You can select from tropical seaweeds as well as imitation kelp from the cold waters of our West Coast. Even artificial corals have been manufactured so that the problems of pollution from improperly cleaned corals and breakage of the delicate branches of real coral are eliminated.

For the outside of the tank there are marine underwater scenes. These come in various sizes to fit the back of a particular sized tank. They add depth to the tank and help portray a typical marine environment. Some are flat and fit up against the back of the tank snugly; others are three dimensional and stick out from the back of the tank a short distance. For those who really want to go all out there is the diarama. This is an underwater scene constructed of whatever materials you want (including those that cannot be placed in the tank) placed *behind* the tank. This of course means that you have to have a platform behind the tank on which it can be placed. Usually the back of the diarama is formed by a curved piece of plastic or cardboard colored black, blue, or green to simulate more natural conditions. This plastic extends from one back edge of the tank to the other and the scene is constructed in the semicircle formed by it. The bottom is usually covered by gravel of the same type as in the aquarium so that there is no abrupt change from inside the tank to the outside. Sea fans, coral, sea shells, or whatever you want can be placed in position so that it is pleasing to the eye when viewed through the tank. The back piece may also

be covered with one of the underwater scenes if you can find one that fits.

Position the corals or other decorations in the main tank so that they are not likely to fall or be knocked over. You can make a pleasing arrangement by placing some large pieces along the back wall of the tank and in the back corners. A centerpiece can be placed in the middle of the tank or just off center. Try to make an arrangement that will enable you to see what's going on in every part of the tank. Many aquarists who have decorated their tanks beautifully but without this in mind have found that they must tear everything down again to find a dead fish or invertebrate that has found a hideaway in which to die. Remember also that you might have to net out a fish or invertebrate because of disease or injury or simply if there is a bully in the tank. In a coral-filled tank catching anything is very difficult. The coral seems to snag the nets almost purposefully as you try to corner the animal you are after.

You can add coral both inside and outside in the back of your marine tank. The coral (facing page) shouldn't be handled as your hands might carry detergent or an insecticide. A coral printed background is a lot less expensive than the real thing.

When setting up your tank be sure your hands are absolutely clean and free of soap, detergent or anything which might poison the tank.

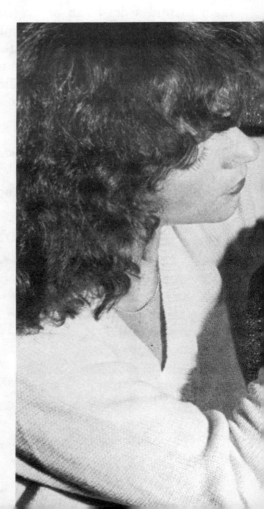

Setting Up Your Tank

Now that you have all the equipment purchased and have a vision of the finished tank in your mind you are ready to begin the actual setting up of the tank. In the chosen location you might want to first place a mat or piece of rug or plastic on which to set the tank. This will protect the floor or carpet from salt water to some extent and can be changed from time to time when a thorough cleaning of the tank is necessary.

The stand is placed in position on the rug (if used) with the idea that it is not going to be moved for a long time. Once the tank is filled with water you would have to empty it again if you decide you want it in another location. The tank is

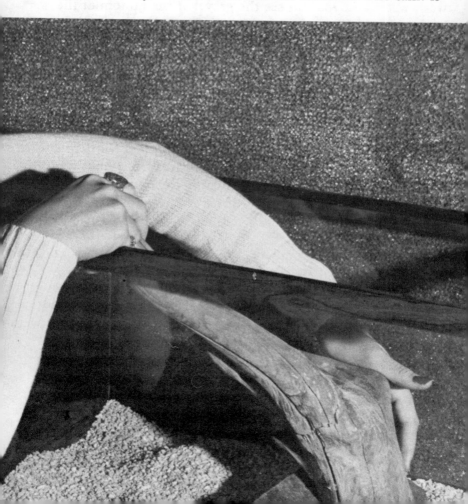

then placed on the stand making sure it fits properly and has adequate support. A foundation for the tank that is not flat will cause the tank to twist a bit, causing abnormal stress on it, and possible cracking or leaking.

Once the tank and stand are in place the undergravel filter (if used) can be added. The tubing for the outlets that lead to the valves and pump can be added later when you have a better idea of the length you will require.

The gravel is then added. Do this by placing some of the gravel in a plastic bucket and washing it thoroughly. It is ready for the tank when no residue is floating about in the wash water and you can see the gravel at the bottom of the bucket clearly a few seconds after stirring it up. Pour off the wash water and dump the washed gravel into your tank. Use your hand to push the gravel around to the best position. It may be best to start at the corners with the first buckets of washed gravel and move forward. Once the basic layer is established you can start grading the gravel so that the higher spots are in the back and along the sides, the lowest spot being in the center front. This will help you siphon out debris as it will tend to collect in the lowest part of the tank. Remember to have enough gravel covering the undergravel filter to a depth of about two to three inches. You can have about three inches in the back grading down to about two in front.

Now for the decorations. Place the decorations in the sand so that they are quite stable. Make sure also that the decorations do not get in the way of the operation of the undergravel filter. In other words, leave enough open space so that the filter can do its job. At this point, too, you can shift the pieces of coral around until you are satisfied with the appearance of the tank. Any items (scenes, diarama, etc.) can be set up at this time to coordinate with the appearance of the interior of the tank.

The water can be added. If you have properly planned ahead you now have thoroughly mixed sea water that has al-

ready undergone any necessary ageing. If not you must now mix the water and wait until it is ready. When the water is ready for the tank you can start adding it a little at a time. If you take a bucketful and just dump it into the tank, you will find that the force of the water has undone all your careful work. It will scatter the gravel in all directions, possibly knock down some of the decorations, and no doubt expose part of the plates of the undergravel filter. To avoid this add the water slowly and preferably pour it onto a solid piece of coral to help soften the blow. As the water level rises the water itself will have a cushioning effect and you can pour a little faster. Keep an eye on the bottom gravel as you add the water to see that it is not displaced to any great extent.

Fill the tank up to near the top, giving yourself some leeway for working on the tank without worry of overflow or spillage. An inch or two below the top of the tank is sufficient.

Set up the airstones, valves, and additional filters. The pump can be placed in the vicinity of the tank on a stand next to it or on a shelf behind it. Be sure that it will not "travel" or move due to the vibration. Disasters have occurred when a pump with all its connections worked its way off a shelf and either crashed to the floor taking various items with it or worse yet fell into the tank and shorted out, electrocuting the animals and sometimes causing an electrical fire. It is also best to situate the pump above the water level to prevent any water feeding back into it and causing damage. There are also filters that fit into the tubing leading from the pump to the airstones or valves for preventing such a backflow.

While connecting the filters and airstones and placing the heater in position, remember that the cover has to fit. Make sure that the heater, tubing, etc., are in the best position for passing through the holes in the cover. Once the heater, filters, and airstones are set up the cover can be put in place.

Plug the appliances in to see how they work, being careful

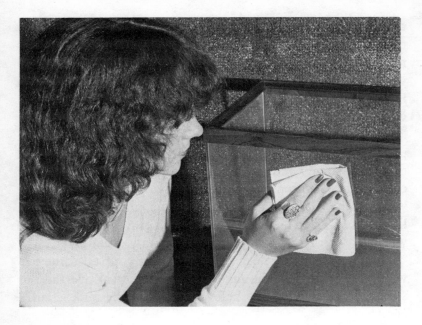

Before setting up your tank, clean it thoroughly with a paper hand towel which has been soaked in salt water. Then add the substrate (below) which has already beeen cleaned. You can even use plastic plants (facing page) in your marine aquarium.

to avoid shocks. Make sure your hands are dry and there is no water spilled on the floor. If you have a bleeder valve leave it open when you first plug in the pump. Once the pump is running you can close this valve slowly until the filters and airstones are running. The individual valves will help disburse the air to the proper items, as the airstones need more pressure to run than does a simple air lift on a filter. This balancing may be quite simple if you are lucky, but it usually takes a bit of juggling to get everything just right.

This is a good time to place a chair in front of the tank and just sit and watch everything for a few minutes. With the aquarium light on this is how the tank will look and operate, and if there is anything wrong or anything you want changed now is the time to do it.

Don't use brass valves, or any brass, with your marine aquarium as the brass (copper) might poison the tank. You should check the chemistry of the water before you add fishes to the tank.

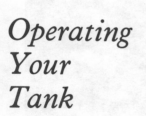

Operating Your Tank

When everything is to your satisfaction and running smoothly, check the chemistry of the water. Although it was correct when you mixed it, it may have been altered by the materials and conditions in the tank. If it has shifted you can adjust it at this point.

MARINE SYSTEMS

There are three basic systems that are advocated by marine aquarists for keeping their animals: the natural system, the sterile system and the biological system. Very few people are

able to keep a natural system going, and it is not recommended for any but the most experienced aquarists. It uses no filtration other than that accomplished by the animals themselves and only a little aeration. The sterile system is what you have now. Except for some minor contamination you should have a perfectly clean tank. The fishes can be added and the cleanliness of the tank kept up by high filtration levels and frequent cleaning of the filter material.

The biological system is the currently accepted method of keeping marine fishes. This is accomplished by inoculating your tank with certain bacteria which will eventually stabilize the chemical conditions caused by decay—at least theoretically. It works like this. Add to your aquarium either some of the filter material from an already established marine aquarium, a bit of chopped clams, or a few hardy fishes that are expendable. You will find that the levels of toxic substances (ammonia and nitrites) increase dramatically, peak, and then drop back down to practically nothing. Here's what's happened. By placing some material from an established tank into your own, you have effectively inoculated your tank with certain types of bacteria. Some of these bacteria are able to take the ammonia produced by decay and change it into nitrites; others are able to take the nitrites and change them into less harmful compounds called nitrates. As the clams you have added to your tank decay or the fishes excrete their waste material, the amounts of ammonia and eventually nitrites increase unchecked. But not for long. The bacteria, suddenly finding plenty of "food," blossom (a real population explosion). But as their numbers increase there is a reduction in the amount of food (ammonia and nitrites) available and therefore their numbers decrease. They become reduced to a number that can adequately handle the amounts of ammonia and nitrites produced in your tank.

You can follow this entire sequence of events with your test kits and your nose. As the decay progresses so does the odor, but as the bacteria take hold the smell decreases pro-

A healthy tank will support a healthy growth of live corals and other invertebrates. The invertebrates are usually the first things to die in an aquarium which is going bad.

portionately. With your test kits you will find that the ammonia level in your tank increases rapidly to a high level quickly followed by the nitrites. The decay has produced the ammonia which in turn was converted to nitrites by the bacteria. As the ammonia is converted to nitrites the ammonia level must of course go down, with a corresponding increase in the nitrite level. But the bacteria convert these newly produced nitrites to nitrates, so the nitrite level drops. It is at this point, when the ammonia and nitrite levels have passed their peak and have dropped to nearly zero, that you can start adding the animals.

The time it takes for all these processes to occur varies depending upon the conditions in the tank, the strength of the bacterial inoculation, the amount of decaying organic matter added, etc. You just have to keep track of the curing of the tank by the tests. Sometimes you can bring the water to your

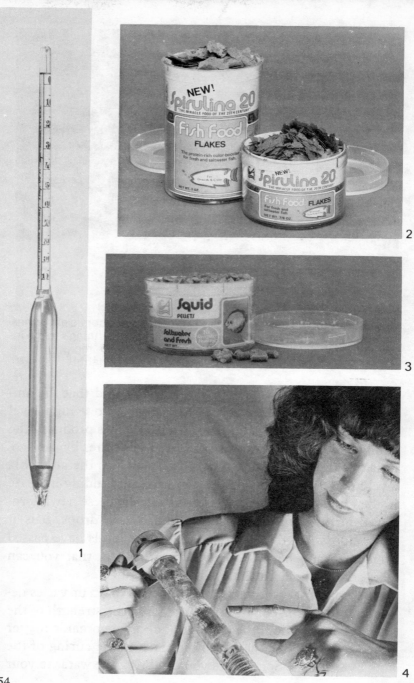

Be sure to bring home a (1) hydrometer; (2, 3) a few kinds of fish food; (4) a non-metallic, non-corrosive heater; (5) a good salt mix with trace elements; (6) an aquarium thermometer; (7) first aid remedies and (8) a trace element revitalizer to replace those elements which are absorbed by the coral and substrate.

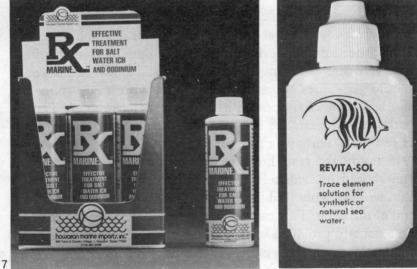

dealer at intervals and have him test it. He will then let you know when the tank is "ready." Most dealers are happy to perform this service since it means that you will probably be buying fishes, invertebrates, or both from him as soon as the tank is safe.

Before going out and purchasing a bunch of animals for your new tank, run a quick check to see that everything is still as it should be. Make sure the ammonia and nitrite levels are down, the pH is about 8.3, the temperature is within the proper range, the salinity (or density) is correct, the airstones and filters are working properly, and no foul smell originates from the tank.

MAINTENANCE

It is unfortunate that many people, when they have set up their aquarium and it looks beautiful, settle back to enjoy it and do not think they have anything more to do than to feed the animals every once in a while. This is a dangerous practice. You must faithfully keep a check on the tank and its inhabitants if you will have any amount of success as a marine aquarist.

First of all set up a schedule of tests. Every week record the pH, ammonia level, nitrite level, and specific gravity. The pH should be about 8.3, the specific gravity about 1.025, the ammonia level less than 0.01 ppm, and the nitrite level less than 0.1 ppm. If you wish to add a nitrate test you should get values of less than 40.0 ppm with hardy animals and less than 20.0 ppm with the more delicate ones. Temperatures can easily be checked with a thermometer at brief-er intervals, perhaps a few times per week.

If any of the tests indicate that conditions are not right, you should immediately set about correcting the problem. You will probably find the pH edging down towards the acid end of the scale. This can be corrected chemically with materials usually provided with the test kit or through a partial change of water. This partial change of water is a good prac-

tice to get into. It removes some of the ammonia and nitrites and replaces some of the trace elements used up by the inhabitants of the tank. It can be done as you siphon out detritus, etc., from the bottom. Continue siphoning until you have removed about 10-15% of the water and replace it with new marine water. This change can be made about every other week (more often if you are having a hard time keeping things in check). If you are having troubles with the chemistry, check to see that the tank is not too crowded, a common practice that often causes these problems.

If you find the specific gravity increasing (as you might with evaporation occurring) add some fresh water to bring it back within the optimal limits.

Check your inhabitants at least once daily to see that they are all alive and well. If one is missing begin an immediate search of the tank—remember I said to position the decorations so that almost all of the tank is visible from the outside? Look around the outside of the tank as well to see if a missing animal has not escaped or jumped out. If the missing animal still is not found, start poking around a bit with a plastic rod or equivalent. Only as a last resort should you start moving corals or other decorations around in your search. This may be a bother, but if this animal has died it is much more of a bother getting the tank back in shape once it starts decaying. If you have found that the animal is dead and have removed it, make an immediate check on the chemical composition of the water. If the ammonia and nitrite levels are much too high, change some of the water immediately. If this does not do the trick you may have to make a larger water change or even a complete water change if things have really gotten out of hand.

Among other scheduled maintenance duties is the cleaning of the outside filter. A replacement of part of the carbon (if used) can be made at that time. Many people use dolomite or similar substances in their filter box as an added hedge against acidification of the water. Do not clean all the filters

(including the undergravel filter) at the same time. It is in the box of the outside filters and the gravel of the under-gravel filters that the bacteria you have so carefully cultured reside. Cleaning everything will kill most of them and you may have to reinoculate your tank again with a fresh culture.

A regular cleaning of the front glass is also recommended. The buildup of algae is so gradual that you might be surprised how much has accumulated in the interval. Tank decorations can also be cleaned on a regular basis. Perhaps the best way is to do only one at a time. This causes less disruption of the tank and is easier to manage. Corals can be cleaned by a strong jet of water from the tap (but be careful it is not strong enough to break the coral) or scrubbing with an old brush.

As your aquarium water evaporates, the salt will remain on everything in the aquarium which extends above the water line. Check the heater and plug carefully to prevent a short circuit. The salt on the glass (facing page) is easily removed with an aquarium scraper, but don't drop the residue back into the water unless you add sufficient fresh (not salt) water to compensate.

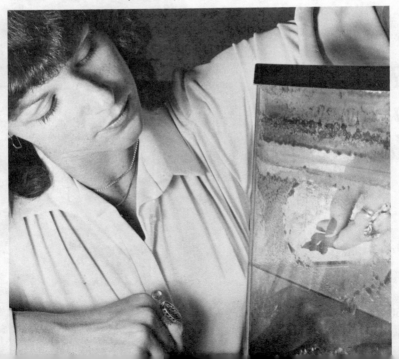

Marine invertebrates are as interesting as marine fishes, if not more so. Your dealer will offer you anemones, live cowries and the like.

The Fishes and Invertebrates

As soon as your tank is set up and operating properly, you are ready to start adding the fishes and invertebrates. Their selection is very important, and you must be familiar with the ones you choose, at least to the extent of knowing which ones will fight with each other and which will eat each other. It has happened that an aquarist has purchased a bunch of animals for his aquarium based purely on what attracted him at the time, only to find out that the predators quickly devoured all the smaller animals and killed some of the others. In other instances aquarists have been rudely shocked when they have purchased (at no small expense) a nice little fish or

invertebrate and placed it in their tank only to see the inhabitants of the tank dispatch it before it even reached the bottom. If you have studied the animals in advance you should be able to avoid such traumatic occurrences. Your dealer will also give you good advice as to which species are compatible. His advice will usually be sound, for he knows he has lost a customer if that customer comes back to tell him one of the animals he just purchased was eaten by one of the others.

INVERTEBRATES VS FISHES

Which type of animals do you want to keep? Normally you have a choice between an all-invertebrate aquarium or an all-fish aquarium. It is only in rare instances that you can mix the two. By far the most popular tank is one which includes only fishes. The invertebrates generally take a back seat to them, as can be seen by the proportion of fish tanks to invertebrate tanks at your dealers. The marine aquarist will often get into keeping invertebrates only after he has maintained fish tanks for some time and is looking for something different. Some people, of course, will keep only invertebrates, which they consider much more interesting than the fishes.

There are some fishes and invertebrates that can be mixed. The best example is the clownfish-anemone relationship. The anemone, an invertebrate, has stinging cells (nematocysts) in its tentacles which help it ward off predators and unwanted guests. Certain animals, the clownfish being the most conspicuous, are able to live among these deadly tentacles, apparently immune to the stings. They are thus protected by the anemone from predation. It has been found that they coat themselves with a mucus which prevents the discharge of the nematocysts. If the clownfishes' body mucus is scraped off, they are stung when placed among the tentacles of the anemone. The immunity will be built up again, but until it is the clownfishes are forced to stay out in the open (unless they can find a hole to hide in) where they